The
HELP
Yourself
(and others)
Cook Book

Dawn Waldron

The Ghana Education Project has provided the stimulus for me
to record and illustrate the recipes and ideas that have
been in my head for some years now.

It's dedicated to my daughter, Polly, and to all the gorgeous
TWGGS girls who before, with and after her are giving their
love, energy and potential to make a difference in Ghana.

This is my contribution to that cause.

Published by Search Press
www.searchpress.com

ISBN 9781844485598

Text, design, layout and illustrations by Dawn Waldron.

Printed in Malaysia.

Why would I buy this book?

For a start you'll be getting 20 fresh, easy-but-interesting weekday suppers that will save you time (I'd lay odds that will more than double your repertoire) and a host of other low fuss meal ideas from healthy breakfasts to easy picnics. It will also provide you with nutritional advice to help your family to be more healthy, while helping you to make sense of the food nonsense that is out there. But the fundamental motivation for writing - and buying - this book is that every penny of the proceeds will go to help the people in Nkwanta in Ghana where subsistence farming is the only means of survival and education is still a luxury that few people can rely on.

This is a proper cook book for people who want to get good food on the table and have a life as well. It's full of cost-effective, quick and simple recipes made with real food. I'm a nutritional therapist, lifelong cook, cancer survivor, wife and mother; so I've got the credentials. I know we're bombarded with often conflicting information about food and that the pressure to get a healthy meal on the table night after night can become more of a chore than a pleasure; and that budgets are sometimes limited. This book is designed to help you put food worries on the back burner: a month of easy recipes that can be repeated and adapted time and again from basic, raw ingredients that are easily obtained. I've worked on the basis that most families enjoy chicken and salmon but not many people eat monkfish and venison on a week day. Almost all the recipes are based around vegetables and lean protein. Lots of them have an Italian or Asian flavour as that's what I like to cook and I figure you probably don't need another recipe for shepherds' pie.

If you're anything like me, you will treat a new recipe with suspicion, expecting it to be complicated and time-consuming. It's not until I've cooked it once or twice that I 'memorise' it and go with the flow. Every recipe in this book is a go with the flow meal that, once you've cooked it for the first time, can be repeated with one eye on the telly.

Because all the money goes to Ghana

The Ghana Education Project

The Ghana Education Project is a registered UK charity looking to support the development of education and associated infrastructure in Nkwanta, a deprived area of North East Ghana. Founder trustee, Gill Norris, a former teacher at Tunbridge Wells Girls Grammar School (TWGGS) has co-ordinated the efforts in Nkwanta on a voluntary basis since she moved to live there in June 2004. Gill was awarded the MBE for her work with young people both in Ghana and in the UK.

The charity works closely with local Ghanaian authorities and teaching groups. They have initiated many schemes to improve the quality of education and resources including: teacher training courses in Science and Maths; a literacy project to help Primary School pupils; container shipments from the UK of school, medical and sports equipment; financed, restored and equipped buildings for education; built the Kyabobo Sports, Arts and Culture centre. Our next and most ambitious aim is to build, equip and launch a brand new School for Girls. Donations are needed for current projects and can be made on www.justgiving.com.

"Education is the most powerful weapon you can use to change the world." Nelson Mandela

Contents

Ghana is a land incredibly rich in natural resources; it exports gold, timber, cocoa, diamonds and bauxite. But subsistence agriculture is still a way of life for most of the population.

Don't Be Afraid!

There's a lot of nonsense talked about food - or nutrition as we call it these days. So much so that we're all living in fear of it and feeling horribly inadequate in the catering department. Not to mention carrying shopping-basket sized burdens of guilt around for all the 'naughty' things we eat. I can clearly remember, as a child in the 1970s, the adults around me discussing the reported story that 'coffee causes cancer'. (Remember that before you order your next double espresso.) Since then the scare stories have never stopped and the confusion is worse than ever.

There have always been lots of crank stories in the media about food. Mr Kellogg had some very weird ideas and there is never any shortage of strange personalities out there putting us in fear of our lives on the basis of what we eat. We need to get things in perspective.

The fact is, the fear is worse than the food.

I'll say that another way. Constantly obsessing about what you put in your mouth is much worse for your health than eating the odd pizza and slice of chocolate fudge cake. The more we worry about food and cooking, allowing fear and guilt to take the place of interest and enjoyment, the more damaging an effect it is likely to have on our health.

I've come to the conclusion that there are only really 5 ways to damage your health with food and they are:

guilt

compensating yourself with food

rewarding yourself with food

mistaking non-food for food

believing that you don't have time to make food

Let's look at the 5 issues one by one:

guilt

There are hundreds of good reasons to feel guilty about the food we eat, but not many of them involve counting calories or grams of fat. If you must feel guilty about the food you eat then think about the bigger issues: global food distribution; the environmental impact of plastic packaging and take away coffee cups; the big supermarkets' pressure on small food producers; the threat of genetically modified food. I could go on...(and frequently do!)

These are the things we should be worrying about. It's not as simple - nor as selfish - as just regretting your last muffin. Channel that energy into something positive that will make a difference. Buying this cook book is a good start because all the money will go to the Ghana Education Project.

compensation

Many of us eat when we feel tired or helpless. It's not just obese people: it's a national habit. The stuff we eat when we feel tired or helpless tends to be non-food. Pizza, cake, chocolate bars, double steamed caramelissimo macchiato with fries: instant gratification to make it all feel better.

Instead of taking time out to relax, walk in the country, phone someone we love or change out of the job we hate, we eat 'treat' food. Often combined with 'treat' alcohol. That way the worries go away. It's a kind of anaesthetic. You fall asleep on the sofa and, before you know it, the alarm goes off again.

This sort of eating is hiding other issues: because you're eating the wrong food for the wrong reasons, it's bad for your health.

A 2000 Population and Housing census records only 19 houses in the Nkwanta district in a population of 150,000, or 24,000 households. 76% of the population of this district lives in rural areas and scattered settlements.

reward

When we're not trying to make ourselves feel better by eating chips, we're celebrating the fact that we feel good or we've done well with pizza! Or something far more sophisticated but no less toxic.

It's not wrong. But it is short-sighted. It's a strange idea to celebrate with things that weigh us down and give us hangovers. There are many ways to celebrate that would make us feel even better... they don't even have to involve food. But celebratory food needn't be non-food... if you see what I mean. It's yet another way that poor food is ingrained in our culture. It doesn't matter occasionally, but if every set-back, every success, every Friday night... is a reason to eat rubbish, you run out of space for the good stuff. And you run out of energy for life.

Modern man having a great time!

non-food

Our vast food processing industry applies advanced biochemistry to bring you the delights of packaged or processed food. It's called 'added value'. They buy the raw materials (usually in high quantity which makes them very cheap, sometimes in low quality which makes them even cheaper) and turn them into meals. This is the added value. They turn food into meals so that you don't have to. And they charge you money for doing that. They have little regard for the integrity of food, they're just interested in getting the food to you before it goes off (which means they remove a lot of the freshness). In fact, you are not really paying for the food, you are paying for their factory and labour. Imagine how cheap those ingredients have to be!

Long life food doesn't help to make long-life humans!

Usually the meal you end up with isn't as nice as the meal you could make yourself and it often has all sorts of things added to that you wouldn't regard as food. But you're happy to pay for it so that you can watch the box, chat on the phone, or sort the laundry while your dinner warms up in the oven.

So much damage is done to food in pursuit of shelf-life and profit that it could fill another book. Hydrogenation, hydrolysation, concentration, sterilisation, radiation, soil-free propagation. Some of these terms are just blinding us with science - while most of them have a detrimental effect on the food. Some of it is non-food that your body is not designed to process.

A basic principle of healthy eating is that you start with raw ingredients. When you shop your trolley will be full of real food that needs a little help to become a meal. That way the nutrients last longer, you know exactly what you're eating, you'll save money and reduce your impact on the environment by cutting out unnecessary packaging.

time warp

I have a rather zany and untested theory that, if we ate only food we'd cooked ourselves from scratch, no one would be fat. If you had to make your own croissants, crisps, muffins, chips, chocolate... in your own kitchen... there wouldn't be time to go to bed, never mind go to work. Calorie consumption would plummet and you'd spend so much time running around in the kitchen that you'd be as thin as a slice of salami.

On the other hand, I've found that cooking basic good food takes hardly any time at all. I know the food processing industry and supermarkets want you to believe the opposite: they want you to believe that they're making your life immeasurably easier by providing 'food' in plastic microwave cartons with cardboard outer sleeves; that they're freeing you up to do bigger and more important things with your life like tantalising your lover, playing games in the garden with your flawless children or climbing Everest in your spare time. Not that you'd have the energy to climb Everest if you lived on processed food - but that's a different matter. It's all a marketing lie. And it's possible you believe it.

The truth is that it's easy to knock up a great supper all by yourself (or if you prefer, with the help of your kids) in 45 minutes, night after night. I've done it now for about 20 years and I'm still finding and inventing new recipes and new short cuts. It's not a chore - it's part of life. While I'm cooking I talk to my daughter; stare out of the window; remember that it's my friend's birthday next week; or simply stick a phone under one ear and chat away to someone while chopping and stirring. That's what this book's about: taking what I've discovered in my years as an enthusiastic cook, scared cancer survivor, professional nutritionist and creative wife and mother, and passing it on for you to cook, develop and adapt to suit you and your own family.

I hope you enjoy it.

About the Recipes

All the recipes are designed to feed 4 people (except for the breakfasts). To make life easier I've colour coded the ingredients for all the recipes into fresh **(green)**, frozen **(blue)** and stored **(orange)** so that you can see at a glance whether or not you can cook that recipe tonight without going shopping.

To help you with planning and shopping for meals, I've also included a list of the ingredients you need to keep in stock to make the recipes.

All the recipes are straightforward and in many places I've suggested some optional ways to get more veg into them - or more pulses, as this is one area that tends to get neglected in a healthy diet.

Finally, there's a rough guide to the good points of each recipe. How many towards your '5 a day'; whether it's low fat, good fat, low carb, high fibre etc. Not all the recipes are nutritional superfoods - sometimes I've included them simply because they're too delicious to leave out.

e.g.
3 a day
low carb

5 a day - it's all relative

This is one of the better food initiatives from the UK government - but I'm shocked by how many people don't eat their 5 a day. All of these recipes are designed to help you do that. In reality however, the concept of 5 a day depends on how much you eat. It's much more helpful to you and your body to think of it as a proportion of your total food intake. Fruit and vegetables should add up to about 50% of your diet. For some of us that's way more than '5 a day'. Also some of that should, ideally, be raw, and no more than half of it fruit. Juices and smoothies are helpful to top up on a bad day but they are foods, not drinks, and should be treated as such.

Getting Organised

Online Allies

If you haven't discovered the joys of online grocery shopping yet, it's time you did. You can do it in 15 minutes flat, just before bedtime; you can shop on Tuesday for meals on Sunday or, and I hate to admit it, you can do what I do and order your Christmas Eve shop on 5th December and then breeze through the party season knowing that it will all arrive on the day and all you have to do is cook it! To make life easy, I also take advantage of the saved lists facility: if you're in a mad rush, you can order enough to survive 5 days by clicking about 3 buttons.

Most of our food is organic and comes from the wonderful Riverford (www.riverford.co.uk). Every week we get a fantastic selection of fruit and veg plus yoghurt, hummus, butter and bread. It all arrives on Thursday, in time for the weekend. They even put real mud on it for you! All our meat comes from reliable local butchers - who know who they're buying from and how it's reared.

Easy Freezy

Your freezer can be a great ally in making meals easy. I bag everything in portion sizes before I freeze it; enough prawns for a risotto, enough salmon for all of us, soup for one. Also frozen ginger (grates easier) is always there along with plenty of frozen fruit such as peeled bananas (great smoothies and instant ice cream), raspberries, blueberries and stewed apples and rhubarb from the garden. And I always have one meal frozen - either a curry or a stew that I've made earlier - for an emergency. Leftover stocks and gravies freeze readily to form the basis of another meal. And, of course there's the obligatory UFO (unidentified frozen object) which has been there since the Christmas before last.

> The annual education budget for a Ghanaian child is £1.50.
> That wouldn't even buy you a skinny latté in the UK!

Cupboard Love

While we're on the subject, I might as well go through my larder (just be grateful I didn't include photos). Although people can be rightly sniffy, tins are a God-send if you know what to buy. Coconut milk makes a curry base, or a quick Thai rice pudding (delicious with sliced mango). Tinned fish makes it easy to eat more omega 3 fats. Tinned pulses are great as a salad base and for bulking out casseroles and soups. One healthy, cheap trick is to replace 50% of the meat in recipes with pulses. Flour (wholemeal, rye, spelt and white), yeast, granulated sugar and salt are always on hand to feed my trusty bread making machine. (We often put a loaf on to cook overnight and wake up to the smell of fresh bread in the morning; it's quicker than popping to Tesco.) Caster and soft brown sugar are in there, but I also keep a Xylitol sweetener in the cupboard which is a natural, low calorie sugar substitute with various health benefits. I use it 50:50 in the few recipes that include sugar. Bottles of flavourings are an easy way to add interest to meals: soy, tamari, and chilli sauce, various oils and vinegars, beat the hell out of those revolting, gunky cook-in sauces. Then there are always some nuts, dried fruits and berries for quick snacks. Sugar free muesli, granola, linseeds, oats, Ryvita, oat cakes, soya milk and UHT milk complete the picture. Oh, and a tin of evaporated milk because it reminds me of my childhood.

The Big Chill

My fridge is the place where I store all sorts of goodies that help me make good food. For a start I store all my veg in the fridge where the high humidity stops it going soft. I also have all sorts of 'flavours' in there: garlic, ginger, chilli, fresh herbs, Patak's curry pastes, preserved lemons. It means I'm never stuck for something to make for dinner.

The list overleaf contains all the ingredients you need to make all the recipes in this book. If you've got them in the kitchen, you can eat tonight.

Always In Stock

FRIDGE

Lots of seasonal veg & salad, butter, free-range eggs, mayonnaise, cheese (parmesan, strong Cheddar, blue, mozzarella, feta, halloumi, cottage), semi-skimmed milk, Alpro soya milk, Patak's curry paste, lemons & limes, herbs, garlic, onions, whole-wheat tortillas, hummus, tahini paste, miso paste, preserved lemons, seasonal berries, natural yoghurt, ghee (clarified butter).

FREEZER

Peas, broad beans, sweetcorn, soya beans (used like peas), bacon, lardons, smoked salmon, haddock and mackerel, portions of salmon, prawns, chicken thighs, organic meaty sausages, naan bread, ginger, berries, bananas (peeled), spare butter, lime leaves, coffee beans.

BOTTLES&JARS

Olive oil (light and extra virgin), rapeseed oil, sesame oil, maple syrup, black olives, roasted red peppers, soya milk, UHT milk, balsamic vinegar, sherry vinegar, rice vinegar, Thai fish sauce, soy sauce, tamari, sweet chilli sauce, pomegranate molasses, basil pesto, red pepper pesto, whole grain mustard, red onion marmalade, lime pickle, peanut butter, Marmite, vermouth, capers.

TINS

Chopped tomatoes, wild red salmon, sardines (lemon, chilli), tuna, chickpeas, borlotti beans, lentils, coconut milk, Whole Earth baked beans.

DRIED

Puy, pardina and red lentils, polenta, brown basmati rice, risotto rice, wholewheat pasta, cous cous, soba and glass noodles, palm sugar, Ryvita, oat cakes, pine nuts, pumpkin seeds, linseeds, raisins, oats, sugar-free muesli, granola, nuts, flaked almonds, dried fruit, bouillon.

HERBS&SPICES

Turmeric, cumin, coriander, cardamom, cinnamon, dried rosemary, garam masala

Readers Digest

There is something magical about food preparation: the smell and sight of food sends signals to your body to get ready to eat. Conversely, if you always turn up at the dinner table in a mad rush, straight from the office, the joys of indigestion are likely to be yours. Digestive juices are strong: neat stomach acid could easily eat through the bonnet of a car… yes, even your ex's Jaguar (stop right there!). So although drinking water is very important for good health, sloshing gallons down with your meal is counter-productive. Aim to sip about half a pint of water with food. And a glass of wine can enhance the acidic environment that aids digestion.

A lot of these recipes contain beans and pulses, although you will be pleased to know that I haven't included a recipe for nut loaf. If you find beans give you wind you may be tempted to steer clear, but try not to. The more your tummy gets used to beans and pulses, the better it deals with them. The health benefits are so great - especially for female hormone balance - that I really think it's worth learning to tolerate these foods.

Chatting with a Nutritional Therapist about digestion

Brisk Breakfasts

Breakfast is a must. Research shows that people who skip breakfast tend to be fatter. It's nonsense, of course, but it helps to support my point :-) However, I do happen to know that people who skip breakfast often make up for it later in the day with foods that are much less healthy.

In my clinic, lots of people tell me that they're just not hungry at breakfast: I tell them they've eaten too much the night before. Ideally, you would digest your evening meal before going to bed. This leaves the digestive tract empty so the body can focus on its overnight detox and repair work. When this happens, you'll find you wake up hungry. So if you can't face breakfast, cut down on dinner! A good breakfast allows you to sweep past the muffins on your way through the coffee shop and arrive at lunch unscathed. So try it.

And answer me this... Why do we all insist on buying skimmed or semi-skimmed milk instead of whole milk? And then we put butter (or even the dreaded 'spread') on our bread?! Full-cream milk is 3 to 4% fat, whereas butter is at least 80%. So one tiny speck of butter (or any other food that has a morsel of fat in it) undoes all the good of avoiding full-cream milk. It's complete nonsense. If you like whole milk, buy it. It might satisfy your appetite enough to allow you to avoid a cheese sandwich at lunchtime. And, to be clear, I've got nothing against butter. It's a great source of vitamin D and healthy short chain fatty acids. Fat is not the enemy!

Absolutely no time for breakfast

1 banana (or an apple, or a pear)
This won't stop you eyeing up the muffins but it will get your metabolism moving and mitigate the risk of you hitting the chocolate fudge cake instead.

The most basic breakfast

A generous slice of wholemeal toast spread with

1 peeled banana sprinkled with

1 tablespoon of pumpkin seeds,

chewed well.

A simply better breakfast

2 tablespoons oats

1 tablespoon linseeds

2 tablespoons muesli or Lizi's low GI granola

(you can keep these ready mixed in a Tupperware if you're sad like me)

handful chopped, seasonal fruit or berries (fresh or frozen)

tablespoon organic natural yoghurt

Before you have your shower (or the night before) soak your dry grains in just enough water, milk or soya milk to cover them. (This helps to pre-digest them and supports your bowel to work properly.) When you're ready to eat it, add the fruit and yoghurt.

If you're not hungry in the morning you ate too much last night.

Or a smoothie

If you prefer to drink your breakfast, place all the above ingredients into a blender with an extra half pint of milk, soya milk or fruit juice and blend until smooth.

A warming breakfast

Make porridge according to instructions. Serve topped with chopped banana and a dessertspoon of maple syrup. Or blueberries and yoghurt. Or prune compote. Or yoghurt and cinnamon. It takes 10 minutes flat, especially if you soak the oats the night before.

"The Digey" brunch

2 per person organic meaty breakfast sausages

2 per person ripe tomatoes

1 per person generous slice of sourdough bread

Cut the sausages in half along their length and place cut side down in a heavy frying pan. Cook them over a medium heat until they are slightly caramelised underneath, turning a couple of times. Set aside. Add the quartered tomatoes to the same pan with a knob of butter and black pepper (and some Lea & Perrins if that does it for you) and sizzle away until warmed and softened. While this is happening, toast your sourdough. Serve tomatoes on toast, drizzled with a little olive oil and sausages on the side. This recipe also works well with mushrooms instead of tomatoes. It's just as tasty as bacon and eggs but much less hassle.

Thanks for the inspiration to The Digey Food Room: a wonderful, warm, wholesome and delicious restaurant in St Ives.

In 2008 an estimated 28.5% of Ghanaians were living below the poverty line. The figure is higher in Nkwanta.

Lazy Lunches

Quick salmon salad

Drain a tin of red salmon in spring water and half a tin of unsalted lentils. Tear up fresh herbs (e.g. parsley from the garden) and toss together. Add 2 tbsp of olive oil, 2 tbsp of lemon juice and serve on top of a green salad. (Makes more than one serving.)

Quick chickpea salad

Drain a tin of unsalted chickpeas. Add an equal quantity of chopped tomato, cucumber, spring onion, red onion, red pepper, fennel, celery (in fact, any salad veg you've got in the fridge). Add a generous handful of chopped herbs and drizzle with olive oil and lemon (or yoghurt and cumin).

Posh sardines on toast

Take 2 thin slices of rye bread and grill gently on one side. Turn over. Spread with tomato puree or red pepper pesto, flake sardines on top and place under the grill for 2 minutes. Pile with rocket and sliced tomato and serve. You could use mozzarella instead of sardines.

Sardines...
the nearest thing to a free lunch!

Posh cheese on toast

Spread a slice or 2 of lightly toasted wholemeal bread with a little butter and a thin layer of mustard. Add a layer of sliced tomato followed by a layer of thinly sliced strong cheese. Grill until bubbling. Serve with some red onion marmalade. You can do the same with pesto, tomato and mozzarella... or stilton and red onion marmalade.

Quick vegetable soup

Sweat a finely chopped onion in water and olive oil in the bottom of a large pan. Throw in handfuls of whatever vegetables you have in the fridge (squash and red pepper; spinach and mushroom; potatoes and leek; sweet potato and broccoli, celery and tomato). Top up with a pint of bouillon stock. Cook until vegetables are tender. Serve as is, or puree with a hand blender.

Quick pea and 'ham' soup

Sweat some bacon lardons, an onion and a clove of garlic in the bottom of a heavy pan. Add a pint of boiling water and about 300g frozen peas (according to your taste). Bring to the boil and whizz with your hand blender to your desired consistency. Serve with some chopped mint and a dollop of yoghurt.

Mega quickie

Grab a raw carrot, 2 Ryvita, half pot of hummus and a handful of raw, skin-on almonds. Eat.

Only time for a quickie?
Ryvita, hummus, carrots and almonds.

Serious Snacks

There's nothing wrong with snacking if you're hungry. But do it properly.
If you don't eat a proper snack, you'll be back again cruising the fridge an hour later. If you find, however, that snacking is stopping you from being able to leave the kitchen, you may have some issues you need to sort out instead. (It's a clue!) Maybe you should get a Sky subscription?

You do need to be careful what you snack on. Sugary/starchy snacks are not good. They can cause mood swings, weight gain, and exacerbate fatigue. They don't last long in the digestive tract which means you are hungry again more quickly.

In fact, although most people think that low fat is the secret to healthy living, few understand that a healthy fat intake is vital to skin and hormonal health so you may be thinner but you'll be a raving old hag. And that's no way to live! Seriously, though, to keep your weight in check, keeping carbs down is so much healthier and more effective than avoiding every speck of fat. It's better for cholesterol levels too.

The secret of a good snack is to include some protein or healthy fats. They satisfy your cravings and keep your blood sugar stable. On page 23 there are a few snack ideas which do just that. Think of it as a mini-meal. Just scale quantities up and down according to how ravenous you are but stick to the principle of combining protein & carbohydrate.

You need a Smeg fridge and a Boden skirt to do this properly

A Word About Water

A few years ago, we were travelling through Kenya and we noticed a very strange field: there were water stand pipes in a grid all across it. I asked a local what it was all about and he said, "It's a new housing area. The idea is that you buy your pipe and construct your home around it."

We can no longer take water for granted in our world. Wars are being fought over it and not until you imagine - or experience - that your only source of water is a shared stand pipe can you really appreciate how good a glass of pure water might taste.

People often say that, when they drink water, it just goes straight through them. In my experience, once you've got into a better water drinking habit, this stops and you find yourself going to the loo as often as you used to and no more.

The best way to understand dehydration is to think about pot plants. In fact, think about 2 pot plants: one is dried out and desiccated and the other carefully tended and well-watered. What will happen if you pour a glass of water into each pot? Strangely, the well-watered plant will drink it all up and the dry plant's saucer will fill up instead. It doesn't make sense...

Human bodies work in a similar way. Dehydrated bodies don't retain water as well as hydrated bodies. You have to make it a habit. (The best way to tell if you're properly hydrated is to check that your urine is almost colourless.)

But beware - you can drink too much water. More than 2 litres a day is not advisable without replacing electrolytes - and increasing your vitamin intake. That's because electrolytes and water-soluble vitamins are flushed out through the kidneys (and skin if you're exercising). So if you lose a lot of water, salts and vitamins, you can't simply replace the water or your chemical balance will go wrong.

good snacks include:

baked beans on toast

(yes, it is a snack if you're really hungry!)

an apple and 10 almonds

2 Ryvita and peanut butter

4 oatcakes and cottage cheese

half an avocado (with cottage cheese if you like)

a chicken drumstick

150g natural yoghurt with berries/seeds/fruit

a cheese and Marmite sandwich

a tin of sardines (the lemon ones are nice)

half a tub of hummus and some chopped raw veg

(carrots, celery, peppers)

celery and cottage cheese

a boiled egg with wholemeal toast

a handful of mixed nuts and seeds

Dehydration can masquerade as hunger so, if you're constantly hungry, try topping up your water levels and see if that helps.

It's not what you cook it's the way that you cook it!

Even healthy foods can lose their nutrient value or become unhealthy through poor cooking...

All fats have a smoke point, a temperature beyond which they change structure and become hazardous to health. For example, ordinary olive oil is safe up to 180ºC (Gas mark 4): above this temperature (that includes most roasts and stir-fries) you should choose coconut, rapeseed or extra light olive oil (definitely not extra virgin), refined avocado oil or clarified butter (ghee). If a recipe tells you to heat the oil first, just warm it: don't allow it to smoke or sizzle - no matter what the recipe says. Adding water or food to the pan keeps the temperature lower (but don't add water to smoking oil). Never heat nut and seed oils - use them only for dressings. Be especially careful with stir fries: stick with stable oils like coconut or refined avocado oil.

For similar reasons, when cooking meat and fish prefer poaching, steaming and stewing to roasting, grilling and frying. Whenever food is browned or crisped, it becomes a source of harm for the body so barbecuing, char-grilling, roasting and frying are far from ideal cooking methods. That doesn't mean you can never eat them make sure you alternate these with other cooking methods.

When you cook vegetables, maximize the nutrients by steaming instead of boiling and keep the cooking time to a minimum. Eat some raw fruit and vegetables each day: coleslaw is a good idea. You can make delicious slaws by finely slicing fennel, carrots, onions, cabbage, beetroot, celery, apples, pears, etc and adding a light dressing using olive oil and balsamic vinegar; sesame oil, soy sauce and lime juice; walnut oil and orange juice. Just keep experimenting...

20 Simple Suppers

Quick kedgeree

200g dry weight brown rice, cooked

2 hard boiled free-range eggs

200g undyed smoked haddock

100g frozen peas

1 finely chopped onion

½ tsp turmeric, ½ tsp cumin

handful of parsley

2 a day
high fibre
very fast

Hard boil the eggs in the same water you cook the rice in. Steam a portion of smoked haddock with some frozen peas. Sweat the onion with half a teaspoon of cumin and half a teaspoon of turmeric in a large flat pan with some olive oil. (It sounds fussy but it can all be done in 10 minutes.) Flake the fish, chop the egg and mix into the pan with the peas, parsley and brown rice. Cook for 5 minutes. Optional: 2 handfuls salad spinach leaves stirred in at the end. Serve with a dollop of yoghurt and green salad.

Simple salade Niçoise

about 8 cooked new potatoes

2 hard boiled free-range eggs

200g green beans, halved

1 Cos lettuce, torn into bite-sized pieces

12 cherry tomatoes, halved

16 black olives

185g tinned tuna or red salmon, flaked

juice of ½ lemon

olive oil

3 a day
good fats
low carb

Slice the new potatoes and hard boiled eggs. Steam the green beans and refresh in cold water. Mix together with the lettuce, cherry tomatoes, black olives and tinned tuna. Dress with lemon juice and olive oil.

Stuffed & roasted red pepper

4 red peppers

4 tomatoes

2 anchovy fillets

2 garlic cloves, finely sliced

mozzarella or feta cheese

olive oil

green salad

toasted pine nuts

polenta

3 a day
good fats
low carb

Slice the red peppers in half and take out the seeds. Quarter the tomatoes and tuck them inside the pepper halves with a snipped up anchovy fillet and 3 or 4 slivers of garlic. Top with a slice of mozzarella or crumbled feta cheese, Drizzle with olive oil and black pepper. Bake for 50 minutes at 180ºC (Gas mark 4). Serve with a green salad, toasted pine nuts and, if you're not worried about carbs, some polenta, brown rice or crusty rye bread.

Smoked salmon frittata

500g new potatoes

200g smoked salmon

8 free-range eggs

2 tbsp dill

100g petits pois

tomato, watercress, spinach

3 a day
good fats
low carb

Thickly slice the potatoes and boil until just tender (about 10 mins). Drain and cool. Cut the smoked salmon into wide strips. Crack the eggs into a bowl, beat until lightly foamy. Stir in the salmon, dill, peas, salt, pepper and any other herbs you may like. Finally stir in the potatoes. Heat a couple of tablespoons of olive oil in a large frying pan, pour in the egg mixture and cook on a low heat for 10-15 mins until the egg is starting to set. Turn the frittata by sliding it onto a plate and flipping and cook for a further 5 mins. Slide back onto the plate and leave to cool for 5 mins before serving. Serve with a tomato, watercress and spinach salad.

Mexican chicken salad wraps

2 grilled or poached chicken breasts (or 4 thighs)

(oh how I wish my thighs were smaller than my breasts :-)

1 tbsp sweet chilli sauce

2 tomatoes, ½ cucumber, 2 celery stalks

(or other salad veg)

4 whole wheat Mexican tortillas

1 avocado

1 tbsp natural yoghurt

juice of 1 lime

green salad leaves

3 a day
good fats
some raw

Tear the cooked chicken into strips and toss in chilli sauce. Finely chop tomatoes, cucumber and celery. Mash the avocado with yoghurt, lime juice and black pepper. To assemble, place a tortilla on a plate, spread with ¼ avocado mixture, layer with ¼ of the chicken, add a generous handful of salad, roll and serve.

Wraps are so popular in our house that we've 'invented' some different themes:

Moroccan

baba ganoush

(Make this dip by sticking an aubergine in a very hot oven until charred. Scoop out insides and mix with tahini, black pepper and lemon juice.)

or hummus, red onion, mint, feta or halloumi, watercress, olives

Italian

mozzarella, tomato, pesto, toasted pine nuts, grilled red peppers and courgettes, rocket, tinned lentils

Indian

roasted red peppers, spinach, minty yoghurt, lime pickle potatoes, chicken chunks sautéed in a little curry paste

Poached egg on Colcannon mash

1 kg potatoes

small cabbage (pointed, hispi or similar)

100g petits pois

butter

6 spring onions

1 tbsp flour

rapeseed oil

4 free range eggs (or 8 if you're hungry)

2 a day
vegetarian
easy

Cut the potatoes into even sized pieces and boil until almost tender. While this is happening shred a small pointed cabbage. Add this and the peas to the potato water for the last 6 minutes of the cooking time. Drain potatoes etc. and mash with butter. Add 6 finely chopped spring onions and some salt and pepper. Form the mixture into 4 flat cakes, coat them in flour and immediately shallow fry them in hot rapeseed oil until browned and crisp on both sides. Serve at once, topped with one or 2 poached eggs. Delicious!

You can spice up the mash with some green chilli or a teaspoon of mustard if you like.

Simple chicken bake

2 large sweet potatoes

1 leek

chicken thighs

basil or red pepper pesto

bouillon

broccoli or Savoy cabbage

3 a day
low fat
fast

Find a simple chicken... It's not difficult... Ours are all a bit thick - but very loveable. No, really, finely slice the sweet potatoes and a leek into rounds, place in the bottom of a small baking dish and half cover with boiling bouillon stock. Rub 4 organic chicken thighs with pesto, place on top and bake at 180ºC (Gas mark 4) for 45 minutes. Serve with lots of broccoli or Savoy cabbage. (You can do the same with fish, but adding it 25 minutes into the cooking time).

Another favourite and delicious 'rub' for roast chicken in our house is a mix of Marmite and marmalade. Try it!

Salmon tikka with lentil dhal

Dhal is one of those things I was scared of cooking until I tried it recently at The Griffin in Fletching - a favourite restaurant - and realised that it is the perfect comfort food. Then I just had to learn:

4 tbsp yoghurt

2 tbsp Patak's tikka paste

4 100g salmon fillets

2 tablespoons olive oil

2 medium onions, finely chopped

1 garlic clove, crushed

50g baby spinach, trimmed, chopped

½ cup fresh mint leaves (optional)

1 tablespoon ground coriander

1 teaspoon ground cumin

1 teaspoon ground turmeric

2 cups red lentils

400g can chopped tomatoes

2 a day
good fats
low carb

Mix the tikka paste with the yoghurt and thoroughly coat 4 salmon fillets. Place in a sealed container and leave for as long as possible (overnight if you can).

Heat the olive oil over a medium heat, add the onions and cook with a pinch of salt* for 5 minutes until soft. Add the garlic, coriander, cumin and turmeric and stir for a further minute before adding the lentils, tomatoes and 2½ cups of cold water. Cover and bring to the boil. Reduce to a slow simmer, stirring occasionally, for 20 minutes or until the lentils are tender.

Meanwhile heat the grill to its highest setting and grill the salmon for 10 minutes on each side. When it's cooked, add the spinach leaves to the dhal and cook for 2 minutes until they have wilted. Serve the salmon on top of the dhal with a minty yoghurt dressing.

TIP: you can alter the ratio of water:tomatoes:lentils until you get a consistency that you're happy with. It should be like a moist puree. You can also stir in yoghurt, other spices and other cooked veg etc. to suit your taste.

* a pinch of salt saves onions from burning.

Oven-baked sausage and mash

2 large red onions

2 tbsp olive oil

½ glass red wine

8 organic, meaty sausages

4 medium sweet potatoes in their skins

natural yoghurt

mustard

broccoli and greens

3 a day
high fibre
easy

Finely slice the onions and place them in the bottom of a roasting tin with the olive oil and red wine. Place the sausages on top. Cook in a 190º (Gas mark 5) oven with the sweet potatoes on a shelf above. After 40 minutes remove the sweet potatoes (they should be soft - if not cook for another 10 minutes). Slit the potato skin and scoop out the insides. Roughly mash with 2 tbsp of yoghurt and ½ tsp of whole grain mustard. Serve a dollop of mash with sausages and onions on top and broccoli and greens on the side.

Instant vegetable curry

selection of veg for roasting

½ preserved lemon

2 tbsp Patak's curry paste

yoghurt

rapeseed oil

brown rice or naan bread

3 a day
vegetarian
high fibre

Curry doesn't get any easier than this! Chop whatever veg you have - potatoes, parsnips, leeks, carrots, squash, courgettes, celery, aubergine, beetroot, tomato, onions - into 3 cm cubes and place in a heavy roasting tin. Chop half a preserved lemon into small pieces and add to the tin along with 2 tbsp of Patak's curry paste (choose the heat to suit your diners), some rapeseed oil, 3 tbsp of water and toss the whole mixture together. Bake in a 180º (Gas mark 4) oven for 40 minutes. When the vegetables are gently caramelised and tender, serve them up with a dollop of yoghurt, some rice or naan bread. If you prefer a wetter curry, you can add coconut milk or tinned tomatoes half way through the cooking time. To bulk it out a bit more, try adding a tin of lentils or chickpeas.

Smoked mackerel & mango salad

1 mango

1 avocado

spinach, watercress and rocket leaves

4 smoked mackerel fillets

olive oil and lemon juice

pumpkin seeds

Slice a mango and an avocado onto a salad of spinach, watercress and rocket. Lightly grill the smoked mackerel fillets and place on top. Make a dressing with olive oil, a little mustard and lemon juice and drizzle over everything. Top with some pumpkin seeds. (This recipe also works well with smoked chicken or fresh prawns.)

Smoked mackerel is a healthy alternative - unless you're a mackerel!

Fresh mackerel & lime pickle potatoes

4 fresh mackerel

600g potatoes (preferably old)

dessertspoon of Patak's lime pickle

watercress

cucumber

tomato

Get your fishmonger to gut some fresh mackerel for you, dry them and place on oiled foil on a grill pan. Chop the potatoes into large chunks and boil for 15 minutes. Drain and mix well with some rapeseed oil, a knob of butter and a dessertspoon of curried lime pickle. Place mixture in a roasting dish on the top shelf and cook in a 200° (Gas mark 6) oven for 25 minutes along with the mackerel. Check the mackerel are cooked all the way through and the potatoes are beginning to brown. Serve with a watercress, tomato and cucumber salad.

Other things to do with mackerel:

Fresh mackerel is just about as good as it gets. It's plentiful in the UK seas, it's full of healthy omega 3 oils and it's cheaper than chips. It's delicious with lime pickle potatoes but it's just as good grilled with:

- mashed sweet potato flavoured with mustard and yoghurt.
- roasted butternut squash and Bramley apple sauce.
- Mediterranean vegetables roasted with garlic, tomato and lemon.
- a big green salad dressed with lemon and ginger dressing.
- stir fry vegetables and noodles with ginger, chilli and mint.
- beetroot, orange, celery and watercress salad with a yoghurt and horseradish dressing.

In Nkwanta, where roads are practically non-existent, cars are owned by about 3% of the population: 4-wheel drive means owning 2 bicycles.

Broad bean and almond pilaf

250g brown basmati rice

200g frozen broad beans

3 shallots or 1 onion

3 finely chopped cloves of garlic

olive oil

1 tbsp cumin seeds

2 tbsp plump raisins

toasted flaked almonds

2 a day
vegetarian
high fibre

Cook the rice as instructed on packet in unsalted water. 8 minutes before the end of the cooking time, add the frozen broad beans and cook until both beans and rice are done. In a large frying pan, fry the finely sliced shallots in some olive oil with a pinch of salt over a medium heat until they are richly coloured and beginning to brown. Add the garlic and keep cooking for a couple of minutes before adding the cumin seeds and cooking for a further minute. Add the cooked rice, broad beans and raisins, stirring over a gentle heat for about 5 minutes until the rice begins to colour. Sprinkle with toasted flaked almonds and serve with natural yoghurt with a little preserved lemon.

Carnivores might like to add chunks of grilled lamb or chicken.

ONE SOUP...

If you're one of those people who thinks soup is only for lunch and not for dinner then I've got some recipes here to change your mind for ever...

Sarah Raven's minestrone

I love Sarah Raven's cook books. There's just the right amount of emphasis on vegetables for me and all the recipes are delicious. This is an amazing soup. I've even served it with lovely bread to posh people coming to supper and they've been properly impressed!

2 onions, chopped

100g pancetta (or lardons)

1 large carrot, chopped

1 celery stick, chopped

3 a day
low fat
high fibre

2 courgettes, chopped

3 large fresh tomatoes (or 225g tin)

100g red cabbage (or cavolo nero, or Savoy)

500ml Marigold bouillon (or chicken stock if available)

good slug of red wine

225g tinned borlotti beans

fresh Parmesan cheese

In a heavy based casserole, sweat 2 onions with 100g chopped pancetta (lardons will do) and 3 tablespoons of olive oil until they are a deep golden colour and everyone is asking what that wonderful smell is. Add the carrot, celery and courgettes, tomatoes and cabbage. Stir well and add the bouillon and a generous glass of red wine, making sure that the liquid covers the vegetables. Cover and simmer for at least an hour, adding a tin of borlotti beans during the last 10 minutes. The soup should look quite rich and thick. If it's watery consider adding some crushed pasta and cooking for another 10 minutes. Adjust the seasoning and leave it to stand for 10 minutes before serving with Parmesan and crusty bread.

...AND ANOTHER SOUP

Lemon chicken soup with PSB

What's PSB I hear you ask? Purple sprouting broccoli... of course. I've borrowed this recipe from Abel & Cole's marvellous 'Cooking Outside the Box' because I love their food philosophy. It's delicious.

1 glug olive oil

2 finely chopped garlic cloves

1 onion, peeled and chopped

400g chicken thighs cut into bite sized pieces

3 mugs of PSB cut into bite sized pieces
(or any broccoli, courgettes, beans etc.)

4 mugs chicken stock (or Marigold bouillon)

2 free-range eggs

juice of 2 lemons

parsley

1 mug of cooked long grain rice

2 a day
low fat
low carb

Heat the olive oil over a medium heat and add the garlic, onion and chicken. Sauté until the chicken has turned white. Add the PSB and continue to sauté for 3 minutes. Now add the chicken stock, cover and simmer for 25 minutes. Remove the soup from the heat, beat the eggs and lemon juice together in a large bowl. Drizzle 2 mugs of the hot soup stock VERY SLOWLY into the bowl whisking consistently so the eggs don't curdle. It will turn creamy. Gradually drizzle the egg mixture back into the soup pot and keep stirring. Do not boil again. Finally stir in the cooked rice and add seasoning and parsley.

IF YOU'VE NEVER SEEN THAT JULIE WALTERS 'TWO SOUPS' SKETCH
HAVE A LOOK ON YOUTUBE

35

Me-too miso

I was a bit slow getting in on the act with miso soup, believing it to be something complicated or strange. In fact, miso paste is simply an excellent savoury base that can be added to lots of dishes and has a range of health benefits. It comes in a variety of colours - most recipes use white miso but they are all delicious. This recipe is simple and endlessly adaptable.

1 kilo of chopped root veg (beetroot, celeriac, carrots)

1 onion quartered

2 garlic cloves

handful of parsley or coriander stalks

1 litre Marigold bouillon

2 tsp white miso

1 green chilli

low fat
hormone-
balancing

Combine the first 5 ingredients in a large saucepan and simmer for 45 minutes. Strain into another pan and add the miso, chilli and lemon juice, adjusting to suit your taste. Do not re-boil (now or after this stage) or the final taste will be bitter.

You now have your basic broth which you can add to a bowl of anything you like, such as:

cooked noodles: glass, buckwheat, soba, etc.

cooked: prawns, chorizo, salmon, scallops, squid, duck, chicken, mushrooms, butternut squash, courgette, broccoli, etc.

raw: shredded mange tout, carrots, courgette, spinach, cucumber, peppers, coriander, basil, mint, chilli, ginger, lime leaves, etc.

3 of my favourite combinations are:

chicken, coriander, red chilli, shredded mange tout

prawns, chorizo, shredded Savoy cabbage

butternut squash, courgette, red pepper, celery

Thai prawn and potato curry

rapeseed oil

1 tbsp Thai green curry paste

2 crushed cloves of garlic

1 tsp chopped lemongrass

1 tsp palm sugar

1 tbsp Thai fish sauce

1 tin coconut milk

1 large potato cut into 2 cm dice

1 sweet potato cut into 2 cm dice

100g frozen peas

100g prawns (thoroughly thawed)

100g chopped red pepper

3 a day
high fibre
speedy

Sweat the curry paste and garlic in a heavy pan with some rapeseed oil. Add the lemongrass, palm sugar, fish sauce and coconut milk and bring to the boil. Add the potato and sweet potato and gently simmer until almost tender. Then add frozen peas, prawns and red pepper. Cook for a further 10 minutes, making sure the prawns are cooked right through. Serve with brown rice and a cucumber salad.

A sweet potato!

Making Perfect Risotto

I was born in Naples and seem to have absorbed a love for the whole Italian food thing. I'm lucky enough to have been taught to cook Italian food in Umbria and Puglia by 3 inspiring chefs. It's not just the food, it's the whole way of life. I love it! And the best thing I ever learned from all that Italian tuition was how to cook risotto.

Risotto is simple to make but difficult to perfect. You could make it your life's work. (There are worse things.) Every time you cook it the risotto will be a little different but once you get the hang of it, this recipe will be an old friend - and a very quick meal. It's the ultimate comfort food and lends itself to all sorts of tastes and flavours. The great thing about risotto is, once you've mastered the basic technique, you've got the blueprint for 100 suppers. So it's 'Buy one, get 99 free'!

buy 1 get 99 free!

First of all you need the right kind of rice: arborio, carnarole or vialone. They are stubby, short-grain rices. Nothing else will do. I've tried making risotto with brown rice and it just doesn't work.

There is one important thing to bear in mind: for the Italians, risotto is closer to a soup than a solid. It is runny and wet - but also creamy and unctuous. It should pour from the pan - not dollop. It's also vital to remember that from the time you stop cooking it the risotto will keep on cooking until it's in your mouth. You need to get that into your head and stop cooking it about 5 minutes before you judge it to be 'ready'. And risotto should be served on a shallow plate - not in a bowl (I know, I know but that's what they say!)

You will need a heavy based pan (a cast iron wok or Le Creuset sauté pan both work well) and a wooden spoon. And another saucepan with about 1.5 litres of boiling stock in it (although I normally cheat and use a kettle and some Bouillon powder). Once you've read this, you're ready to start.

Pepper and squash risotto

2 red peppers

500g butternut squash

1 red onion

olive oil

1 tbsp balsamic vinegar

1 red chilli (or to taste)

fresh rosemary

2 crushed and chopped cloves of garlic

200g arborio or carnaroli rice

100ml white wine or vermouth

1 tsp bouillon powder (if you're not using stock)

20g butter

parmesan to serve.

2 a day
or more
delicious!

Chop the pepper, squash and half the onion – keeping them fairly chunky. Toss in olive oil with balsamic vinegar, chilli and rosemary. Roast in the oven at 200° C for 40 minutes.

Meanwhile, boil 2 litres of water or stock if available. Gently heat 2 tbsp olive oil in a large, heavy-bottomed frying pan or casserole. Chop the remaining half onion finely, place in pan with the garlic and soften. Add the rice, increase the heat and stir until glossy (1 minute). Add white wine or vermouth. As this starts to evaporate, add a cup of boiling water and the bouillon powder and keep stirring. Continue adding boiling water and stirring, keeping the risotto at a sloppy, flowing consistency and the heat high for 20-30 minutes, until the rice is soft but retains a chalky 'bite' in the centre. Remove from heat and allow to sit for 5 minutes, then beat in a generous knob of butter. Remove the roasted veg from oven and scatter on top of the risotto. Shave parmesan on top. Serve with a green salad. (It's also delicious with a few cubes of blue cheese added at the last minute.)

Variations on a theme:

For endless variations on the risotto theme, leave out the squash and red pepper section in the recipe above and substitute with anything you like. Here are 2 of our favourites:

GREEN RISOTTO

Steam the contents of a large bag of spinach and 200g of peas until the spinach is wilted. Place in a deep jug, add a knob of butter and process to a puree with a hand blender. 5 minutes before the end of the risotto cooking time, stir in the puree. You will have a bright green mess that looks disturbingly like a cow-pat but it tastes divine and feels like a week on a health farm. Serve it quickly before you lose the bright green colour. Sprinkle some feta on top if you must.

PRAWN, BROAD BEAN AND ROCKET RISOTTO

Take some juicy prawns, steamed broad beans and a couple of handfuls of rocket (the small, wild variety if you can get it) and stir them all into the risotto during the last 5 minutes of cooking time. Heat through thoroughly. Serve with shaved pecorino cheese.

Fish pie pasta

This is a recipe with all the flavour of a fish pie and all the simplicity of a pasta dish;12 minutes from start to finish.

300g wholewheat penne

2 tbsp chopped parsley

1 hard boiled egg, chopped

1 dessertspoon capers, chopped

zest and juice of half a lemon

2 generous tbsp creme fraiche or yoghurt

tomatoes

red onions

200g salmon fillet (fresh or smoked) cut into fine strips

2 a day
good fats
high fibre

Cook the penne as instructed in slightly salted water. Meanwhile assemble all the other ingredients except the fish in a bowl and combine. When the pasta is cooked, drain well and quickly add the salmon to it, stirring so that the residual heat of the pasta 'cooks' the salmon. Then stir in the rest of the ingredients. Serve with a tomato and red onion salad.

The best salad ever
(also known as Vietnamese chicken salad)

1 red chilli, seeded and minced

1 garlic clove, crushed

2 tbsp lime juice

1 tbsp (palm) sugar

1 tbsp Thai fish sauce

2 tbsp sesame oil or other oil

2 tsp rice vinegar

3 a day
good fats
high fibre

Combine all the above ingredients and let them sit for half an hour.

200g white cabbage, finely shredded

200g cooked chicken, torn into fine strips

100g carrot, finely grated

1 small onion, finely sliced

large bunch of mint, roughly chopped

Meanwhile prepare and combine all the ingredients above.

Thoroughly toss all the ingredients together and serve. You won't be able to leave any in the bowl.

The dressing can be used for lots of other dishes to add a Vietnamese flavour to salads and vegetables.

More than 70% of the Ghanaian population are not literate. School attendance is poor and, although it is free, many children do not complete their education. Only a handful of schools have power and none have computers. The annual education budget per child amounts to £1.50. The statistics for Nkwanta are much worse than for the Ghanaian population as a whole.

A Fresh Formula

Don't get stuck in a rut with salads. There are loads of options for a main meal salad and it's easy to add some protein on the side - or even tossed in with the rest of the ingredients. Don't be scared either of adding hot ingredients to a cold salad. Sometimes the contrast - and the slight wilting that can occur, especially if you use spinach as a base - is delicious. Mix and match your own salads using some foods from each column:

Base + Texture + Taste

Base	Texture	Taste
Cos	raw broccoli	fresh herbs - chives,
rocket	raw cauliflower	basil, mint, coriander
Romaine	raw fennel	rosemary, thyme etc.
spinach	raw cabbage	garlic
chicory	grated beetroot	blue cheese
little gems	grated celeriac	parmesan
mizuna	carrot batons	feta
Chinese leaves	cucumber	crispy bacon
lamb's lettuce	celery	prawns
mustard leaves	raw peas	anchovies
grated carrot	broad beans	ripe tomatoes
grated beetroot	cooked new potatoes	lemon or lime juice
courgette ribbons	roasted squash	sesame oil
onions - sliced leeks,	asparagus	capers
red onion, spring onion	croutons	olives
cooked pasta	mange tout /	mustard
cooked rice	sugarsnap	cooked chorizo
beans & lentils	roasted red peppers	grapefruit
	avocado	orange
	eggs (quail or hens')	mango
	pumpkin seeds	yoghurt
	toasted nuts	

see salad dressings on the next page...

All Dressed Up...

Having assembled your salad, you might want to dress it up a bit. As a rule, the more complex the salad, the simpler the dressing should be. Often a little lemon juice and a drizzle of extra virgin olive oil is all you need. But a great dressing can transform a dismal salad into a feast. I like to serve salads with all types of cuisine so I slant the taste of my dressing towards the style of food I'm cooking. Here are a few ideas:

French Dressing

1 tbsp wholegrain mustard

1 tbsp red wine vinegar

100ml extra virgin olive oil

1 crushed clove garlic

Italian Dressing

1 tbsp pesto

½ tsp white balsamic vinegar

100ml extra virgin olive oil

1 crushed clove garlic

Moroccan Dressing

handful chopped coriander

¼ preserved lemon

100ml natural yoghurt

1 crushed clove garlic

Thai Dressing

1 tbsp soy sauce

2 tbsp lime juice

50ml sesame oil

½ tsp honey or palm sugar

Indian Dressing

1 tbsp chopped mint

2 tbsp chopped cucumber

100ml natural yoghurt

1 crushed clove garlic

Spanish Dressing

1 tbsp sherry vinegar

juice & zest of half an orange

100ml extra virgin olive oil

1 crushed clove garlic

The Perfect Picnic

I don't know about you but my heart sinks when anyone mentions a picnic. It's not that I don't enjoy having a relaxing afternoon in the sunshine eating lovely food… it's the fact that preparing it normally feels like the equivalent of preparing 3 dinner parties for 12. (That, and the near marital breakdown that takes place as you drive round for an hour-and-a-half looking for a suitable place to stop and eat!) With all that in mind, I've devised a 9-item easy picnic that assembles quickly and tastes delicious.

Marriage guidance: if you're planning a picnic – go out the week before to find the right place to eat, then you can go straight there on the day. It avoids so many rows!

…and lashings of ginger beer!

the perfect picnic contains:

egg mayonnaise and rocket sandwiches
on thinly sliced sourdough.

(make your egg mayo with an equal mix of mayo
and natural yoghurt. Add a little whole grain
mustard and black pepper.)

cold, browned organic chipolata sausages

home grown baby tomatoes
(or supermarket baby plum tomatoes)

tub of hummus or guacamole

carrot sticks

big plate of skin-on chunks of melon and pineapple to eat
with fingers

a sufficient quantity of high quality chocolate

old fashioned lemonade

a bottle of chilled white wine

Remember also to pack:

picnic blanket, cushions, sunshade, sunglasses,
sun cream, sun hats, cutlery, crockery, glasses,
mineral water, corkscrew, wine chiller, kitchen roll,
frisbee, newspaper, books, bottle of washing water and
wash cloth, towel, loo roll, rubbish sack, the dog, the map.

The Molecule of Love

I don't really do puddings. I'm not a zealous nutritionist but I do try to minimise sugar. I really hate the way we set up our children to crave sugar for life by relentlessly shovelling something sweet down their throats after every meal from the minute we start weaning them. I've heard it said that if we tried to introduce sugar into the food chain today the Food Standards Authority would refuse on the basis it's a Class-2 drug. It's addictive and damaging. The less we eat, the better we feel.

That said, we all love a sweet treat every now and again. Preferably not every day. But definitely on your birthday. As well as sugar, chocolate contains phenylalanine - a brain chemical produced when you're in love. (That explains why we sometimes prefer it to our husbands then.)

Cocoa beans make up 16% of Ghana's exports. They were first introduced into Ghana in 1878 by Tettah Quarshie. In the mid-60s Ghana was the world's largest cocoa producer. They export the entire crop and cocoa smuggling is punishable by death.

Here's a truffle recipe that you will love. Make them for the people you love; make them for yourself when the people you love are driving you mad; make them instead of eating shop-bought sweet rubbish.

Tiramisu truffles

Tira mi su means 'pick me up' in Italian. Break 200g of 70% fair trade organic dark chocolate into chunks. Warm 150ml double cream in a small saucepan and bring to a simmer. Take it off the heat and add the chocolate. 'Melt' half a teaspoon of good quality instant coffee in a drop of boiling water and add to the mixture (and a tablespoon of Tia Maria, brandy or Marsala if you like). Stir until you have a smooth mixture. Transfer it to a bowl, cover and leave overnight (if you can!). Next day roll the mixture into little balls and, just before you eat them, roll them in cocoa powder. You can add spice flavours instead of coffee (chilli, cinnamon, cardamom) or roll them in toasted nuts as well as cocoa.

A Simple Diet

Nearly every female I know obsesses about her body. Some publicly, some privately. Some of us hate our whole bodies, while some single out specific parts that we'd like to amputate. Very few of us are happy with the way we look and most of us have a slightly strange relationship with food as a result. In fact the popular idea that we have a 'relationship' with food is bizarre.

If you put 'weight loss diets' into Amazon, you get 3,506 hits in books alone. Two things strike me about this.

a) Why do we need 'a book' to tell us in mind-numbing detail exactly how to eat less? (Try speaking to someone in Nkwanta about that...)

b) While we are all focussed on the size of our thighs, the planet is slowly grinding to a halt.

So, to counteract all the wasted paper and wasted energy that is the 'diet industry' I've designed a simple diet. It works*, I've done it. (But not for long enough!)

All you do is cut out sugar, white flour, potatoes & alcohol...

...and then base your diet around healthy foods: lean meat and fish, vegetables, fruit, whole grains, pulses, nuts and seeds. This rules out nearly all the 'bad' foods known to man and your body will love you for it. It's a simple diet but it's very effective. It takes willpower at first and you need to read the food labels. You might find that you suffer from some serious sugar (and maybe alcohol) cravings in the first 4 days but plan lots of nice things to distract yourself. After that you will feel better than you've felt for some years and you'll find that your energy levels are amazing. You can do this for 6 months to get to your ideal weight (you can do it for life if you want to, it won't harm you). Or you can do it for a month to shed a few pounds.

It sounds too simple to be true but it works. That's because you are cutting out the most calorie-dense but nutrient-poor foods in your diet and their by-products. Plus avoiding alcohol keeps calories even lower and resolution higher. Simple.

*If you are diabetic talk to your GP before dieting as it affects your medication.

Drowning in Plastic

If you want to stay healthy, reduce the plastic in your life – and I don't mean credit cards. Our reliance on plastic is quite possibly at the root of many of the hormone related cancers that are destroying so many of the people we love. If not at the root, they are clearly a part of the problem.

It works like this. We value plastic because it's bendy and waterproof – making it a fantastic way to pack food and drink. This now means we can eat and drink on the street (your grandmother would be scandalised), eat meals cooked by people we don't know, bought from a supermarket, and catch up on the gossip by the drinks machine at work. A great invention.

However, the chemicals that make plastic bendy play havoc in our bodies. They are hormone analogues (which means they can lock on to the same receptors that our own hormones use) and they can exert a powerful effect. These chemicals are released every time we cool or heat the plastics that we store our food in. They are fat soluble which means they leach into fatty foods when they come into contact with them. Oestrogenic in nature they give proliferative messages to our cells and send our natural growth signals into confusion and can lead to cancer.

Just think about how much contact you have with warm or cooled plastic: we drink hot drinks from the drinks machine; we buy lattés in plastic coated cups; we heat food in the oven and microwave in plastic containers; we drink from plastic water bottles all the time (sometimes we even freeze them to access cold water all day – aaarrrgh!) and don't think twice about eating prepared salads, sandwiches, mayonnaise, cheese, oils, etc. etc. that have been stored in plastic packaging.

There is now strong evidence to link breast cancers with bottled water intake and it's time to take this threat seriously. Even NHS cancer centres are issuing warnings about it and they're normally the last to react.

To reduce your reliance on plastic:

> **stop drinking out of plastic cups: take a china mug to work.**
>
> **use a glass or metal bottle to carry water around. If you're worried about breaking it, slip it inside a sock!**
>
> **never heat food in plastic containers – tip it into Pyrex first.**
>
> **use greaseproof paper in place of cling film.**